Especially for

_____

From

_____

Date

_____

© 2011 by Barbour Publishing, Inc.

Compiled by Kathy Shutt.

ISBN 978-1-61626-198-6

Scripture quotations marked KJV are taken from the King James Version of the Bible.

Scripture quotations marked NIV are taken from the HOLY BIBLE, NEW INTERNATIONAL VERSION®. NIV®. Copyright © 1973, 1978, 1984 by International Bible Society. Used by permission of Zondervan. All rights reserved.

Scripture quotations marked NRSV are taken from the New Revised Standard Version Bible, copyright 1989, Division of Christian Education of the National Council of the Churches of Christ in the United States of America. Used by permission. All rights reserved.

Scripture quotations marked MSG are from THE MESSAGE. Copyright © by Eugene H. Peterson 1993, 1994, 1995, 1996, 2000, 2001, 2002. Used by permission of NavPress Publishing Group.

Scripture quotations marked NLT are taken from the Holy Bible, New Living Translation, copyright © 1996. Used by permission of Tyndale House Publishers, Inc. Wheaton, Illinois 60189, U.S.A. All rights reserved.

Published by Barbour Publishing, Inc., P.O. Box 719, Uhrichsville, Ohio 44683, www.barbourbooks.com

Our mission is to publish and distribute inspirational products offering exceptional value and biblical encouragement to the masses.

Printed in China.

Little Whispers of
Blessing
for
Moms

BARBOUR
PUBLISHING

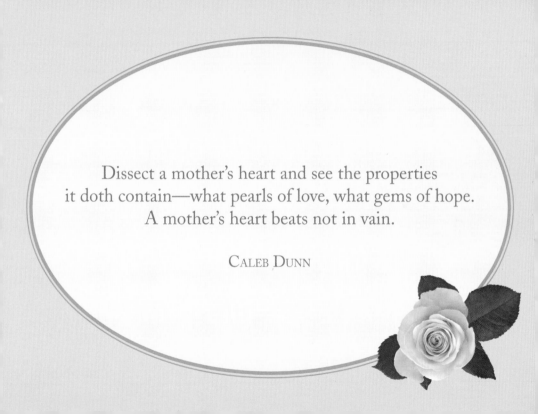

Dissect a mother's heart and see the properties
it doth contain—what pearls of love, what gems of hope.
A mother's heart beats not in vain.

CALEB DUNN

There's only one pretty child in the world, and every mother has it.

Chinese Proverb

Home is where the heart can bloom.

CHARLES SWAIN

A mother understands
what a child does not say.

JEWISH PROVERB

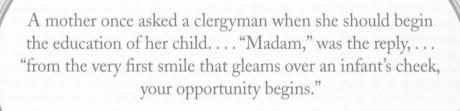

A mother once asked a clergyman when she should begin the education of her child. . . . "Madam," was the reply, . . . "from the very first smile that gleams over an infant's cheek, your opportunity begins."

RICHARD WHATELY

*When God thought of Mother,
He must have laughed with
satisfaction and framed it
quickly—so rich, so deep,
so divine, so full of soul, power,
and beauty was the conception.*

HENRY WARD BEECHER

Have you truly given your children to God?
We trust God with everything in our lives;
but when it comes to our children, we want to
take care of them. But being in the center of God's
will is the safest place a person can be. Giving your
kids to God is the best thing you can do for them.

MICHELLE MEDLOCK ADAMS

The tie which links mother and child is of such pure and immaculate strength as to be never violated.

WASHINGTON IRVING

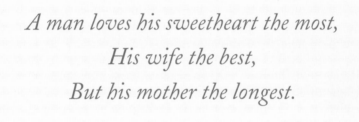

A man loves his sweetheart the most,
His wife the best,
But his mother the longest.

IRISH PROVERB

Children and mothers
never truly part,
Bound in the beating of
each other's heart.

CHARLOTTE GRAY

You should be known for the beauty that comes from within, the unfading beauty of a gentle and quiet spirit, which is so precious to God.

1 PETER 3:4 NLT

Who takes the child by the hand
takes the mother by the heart.

DANISH PROVERB

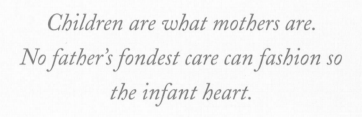

Children are what mothers are.
No father's fondest care can fashion so
the infant heart.

W. S. LANDOR

No joy in nature is so sublimely affecting as the joy of a mother at the good fortune of her child.

JEAN PAUL RICHTER

Why did God make mothers?
To teach us how to love Him. . .
To teach us how to love.

LARISSA CARRICK

Praising the Lord is one of the best things you can do to encourage yourself. Even if you're feeling down when you begin singing, before long, your heart will be glad. Scripture says our tongues should rejoice, so let your tongue rejoice today. Let your kids see you rejoicing in the Lord and before long, they'll join in. It's contagious!

MICHELLE MEDLOCK ADAMS

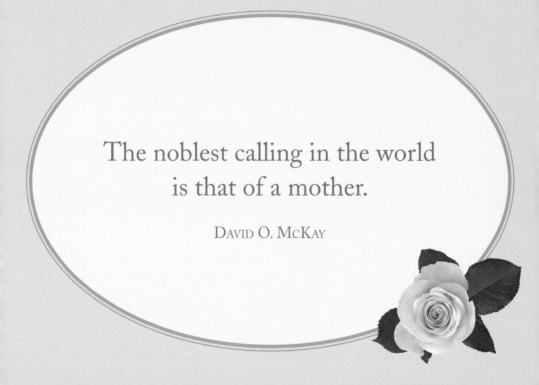

The noblest calling in the world
is that of a mother.

David O. McKay

Pride is one of the seven deadly sins; but it cannot be the pride of a mother in her children, for that is a component of two cardinal virtues—faith and hope.

CHARLES DICKENS

Mother's love is peace.
It need not be acquired,
it need not be deserved.

ERICH FROMM

God pardons like a mother, who kisses the offense into everlasting forgiveness.

HENRY WARD BEECHER

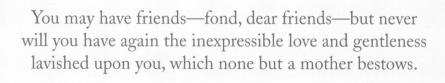

You may have friends—fond, dear friends—but never will you have again the inexpressible love and gentleness lavished upon you, which none but a mother bestows.

THOMAS BABINGTON MACAULAY

The power of one mother's prayers could stand an army on its ear.

ELIZABETH DEHAVEN

Maternal love:
a miraculous substance
which God multiplies
as He divides it.

VICTOR HUGO

A child's hand touches yours—what tenderness and power it arouses. You are instantly the very touchstone of wisdom and strength.

MARJORIE HOLMES

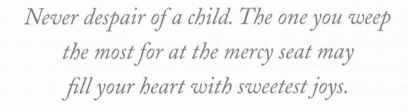

*Never despair of a child. The one you weep
the most for at the mercy seat may
fill your heart with sweetest joys.*

T. L. CUYLER

Children are a gift from the LORD;
they are a reward from him.

PSALM 127:3 NLT

Keeping all of the balls in the air is tough. In fact, some days it seems practically impossible. But on those days, I look to God. He says I can do all things through Him, so I'm holding Him to that. You should do the same!

MICHELLE MEDLOCK ADAMS

A child is a gift whose
worth cannot be measured
except by the heart.

THERESA ANN HUNT

The three most beautiful sights:
a potato garden in bloom, a ship in sail,
a woman after the birth of her child.

IRISH PROVERB

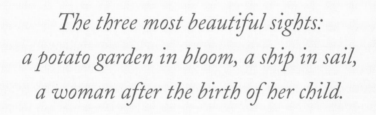

Nothing else will ever make you as happy or as sad, as proud or as tired, as motherhood.

ELIA PARSONS

When there's love at home,
there is beauty all around.

UNKNOWN

How do you start your mornings?
Do you spring out of bed, praising the Lord with
great expectation? Begin each day thanking God.
It will take practice, but you'll get the hang of it.
Let your children see you praising Him,
and encourage them to join you. If you do,
mornings around your house will be a lot brighter.

MICHELLE MEDLOCK ADAMS

Children are the sum of what mothers contribute to their lives.

UNKNOWN

Mother, you carved
no shapeless marble
To some high soul design,
But with a finer sculpture
You shaped this soul of mine.

THOMAS FESSENDEN

A mother's love is like a circle. It has no beginning
and no ending. It keeps on going around and around,
ever expanding, touching everyone who comes
in contact with it.

UNKNOWN

We all encounter difficult parenting moments—embarrassing public tantrums and fits—but if we can keep things in perspective, we'll lead much more joyful lives. Don't let Satan steal your joy, no matter how ugly it gets. Just smile and praise the Lord for every parenting moment—good and bad.

MICHELLE MEDLOCK ADAMS

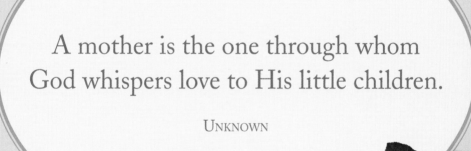

A mother is the one through whom
God whispers love to His little children.

UNKNOWN

*There is nothing so strong as
the force of love; there is no
love so forcible as the love of an
affectionate mother to her child.*

Elizabeth Grymeston

The God to whom little boys
say their prayers has a face
very like their mother's.

James M. Barrie

Romance fails us—and so do friendships—
but the relationship of Mother and Child
remains indelible and indestructible—
the strongest bond upon this earth.

THEODORE REIK

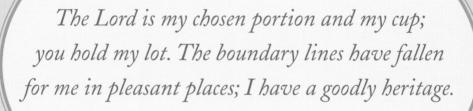

The Lord is my chosen portion and my cup;
you hold my lot. The boundary lines have fallen
for me in pleasant places; I have a goodly heritage.

PSALM 16:5–6 NRSV

I'm so thankful that God is gentle and merciful when He disciplines. He makes His children want to run to Him, not away from Him. No matter how badly we mess up, He forgives and forgets. If you are struggling with being too harsh with your children, ask God to help you. He will pour His unconditional love into you so you can pour that love on your children.

MICHELLE MEDLOCK ADAMS

A mother's love and prayers
and tears are seldom lost on even
the most wayward child.

A. E. Davis

Children need love, especially
when they do not deserve it.

HAROLD S. HULBERT

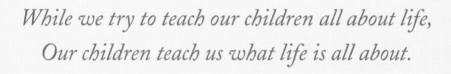

While we try to teach our children all about life,
Our children teach us what life is all about.

ANGELA SCHWINDT

If your day is hemmed with prayer, it is less likely to come unstitched.

UNKNOWN

What a relief to simply let go of my need to do everything perfectly—and instead just do everything for You, [God]! You know I'll always make mistakes; You know that sometimes my best efforts will look like failures to everybody else. Thank You that I can simply relax and trust You to work everything out according to Your plan.

DARLENE SALA

We busy moms rarely take time for our friends.
But we need friends. If you haven't taken time lately
to tell your friends how much you appreciate them,
why not tell them today?
While you're at it, tell your children how much you
value their friendship, too. As my girls get older,
I realize how blessed I am to have their friendship.
Go ahead, reach out to a friend today.

MICHELLE MEDLOCK ADAMS

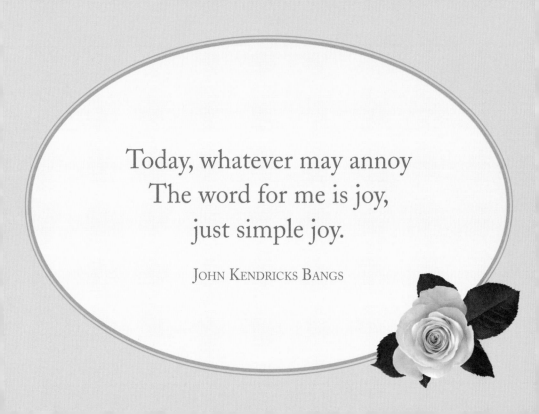

Today, whatever may annoy
The word for me is joy,
just simple joy.

JOHN KENDRICKS BANGS

[Your children] may forget what you said, but they will never forget how you made them feel.

CARL W. BUECHNER

The better you become acquainted
with God, the less tensions you feel
and the more peace you possess.

CHARLES L. ALLEN

A child's kiss
Set on thy sighing lips, shall make thee glad;
A poor man served by thee, shall make thee rich;
A sick man helped by thee, shall make thee strong;
Thou shalt be served thyself by every sense
Of service which thou renderest.

ELIZABETH BARRETT BROWNING

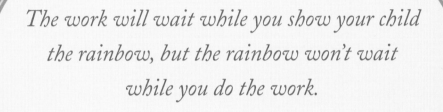

The work will wait while you show your child the rainbow, but the rainbow won't wait while you do the work.

PATRICIA CLAFFORD

*We can't form our children
on our own concepts; we must
take them and love them as
God gives them to us.*

JOHANN WOLFGANG VON GOETHE

Busy days are best organized by God.

PAMELA MCQUADE

Thanks be to God for his indescribable gift!

2 Corinthians 9:15 niv

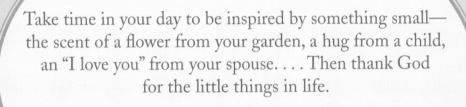

Take time in your day to be inspired by something small—
the scent of a flower from your garden, a hug from a child,
an "I love you" from your spouse. . . . Then thank God
for the little things in life.

FROM *IN THE KITCHEN WITH MARY AND MARTHA:*
ONE-DISH WONDERS

Mothers. . . Remember, when you rock your babies and sing a lullaby, your arms and voice are God's. When you do load after load of dirty diapers and then grass-stained play clothes and finally school clothes smeared with ketchup and chocolate pudding, remember, your hands are God's hands. . . . Through you, He will imprint Himself on your children's hearts.

ELLYN SANNA

Enjoy the little things, for one day you may look back and discover they were the big things.

UNKNOWN

*Being a full-time mother is one
of the highest salaried jobs. . .
since the payment is pure love.*

MILDRED B. VERMONT

Be as a bird perched on a frail branch
that she feels bending beneath her, still she sings
away all the same, knowing she has wings.

VICTOR HUGO

Mothers are like fine collectibles—as the years go by, they increase with value.

<small>UNKNOWN</small>

The time to be happy is now;
the place to be happy is here.

ROBERT G. INGERSOLL

You are blessed. Send up praise to the Father for your children, your spouse, your home, your extended family, your friends. God loves sending blessings our way—especially when we appreciate the ones He's already sent.

MICHELLE MEDLOCK ADAMS

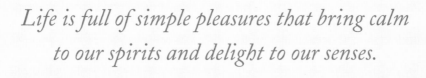

*Life is full of simple pleasures that bring calm
to our spirits and delight to our senses.*

EMILIE BARNES

I long to accomplish great and noble tasks, but it is my chief duty to accomplish humble tasks as though they were great and noble. The world is moved along not only by the mighty shoves of its heroes, but also by the aggregate of the tiny pushes of each honest worker.

HELEN KELLER

You always win a better
response with love.

HELEN HOSIER

Before me, even as behind,
God is, and all is well.

JOHN GREENLEAF WHITTIER

Words of praise, indeed, are almost as necessary to warm a child into a genial life as acts of kindness and affection. Judicious praise is to children what the sun is to flowers.

CHRISTIAN NESTELL BOVEE

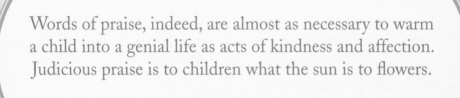

For blessings of the
fruitful season,
For work and rest,
for friends and home,
For the great gifts of thought
and reason—
To praise and bless Thee,
Lord, we come.

ELIZA SCUDDER

Pleasant words are a honeycomb,
sweet to the soul and healing to the bones.

PROVERBS 16:24 NIV

Thank You, Lord, that we may know that our need is never greater than the Helper.

CORRIE TEN BOOM

Love is most divine when it loves according
to needs and not according to merit.

GEORGE MACDONALD

Grace means God accepts me just as I am. He does not require or insist that I measure up to someone else's standard of performance. He loves me completely, thoroughly, and perfectly. There's nothing I can do to add or detract from that love.

MARY GRAHAM

A three-year-old child is a being who gets almost as much fun out of a fifty-six-dollar set of swings as he does out of finding a small green worm.

Bill Vaughan

*Giving seems to be the very essence of
motherhood. So many calls in the night,
so many demands in the day, so little time
for oneself, and so much to give. . .
There is One who gave and who gives
more than any mother. And how mothers
need that which He has to give. . .*

DORIS COFFIN ALDRICH

Has God been there for you when no one else was around?
Has He helped you make it through a difficult situation?
Maybe you're in a tough place now and need His touch.
Just reach out—He's right there. No matter what your
situation—He has the way out. He is able. He is willing.
And He is faithful.

MICHELLE MEDLOCK ADAMS

*Dear Lord, thank You for
my home. I ask that You fill it
with Your Holy Spirit.
Even when I don't have time to
polish and dust, may it still shine
with Your welcome and love,
so that whoever comes in my doors
senses that You are present.*

ELLYN SANNA

A hundred years from now, it will not matter what my bank account was, the sort of house I lived in, or the kind of car I drove. But the world may be different because I was important in the life of a child.

UNKNOWN

Make a list of all the things for which you're thankful. Write it on pretty stationery and display it on the refrigerator where you'll see it often—a daily reminder of everything that's good in your life.

FROM *IN THE KITCHEN WITH MARY AND MARTHA: ONE-DISH WONDERS*

If a child is to keep alive his inborn sense of wonder,
he needs the companionship of at least one adult who
can share it, rediscovering with him the joy, excitement,
and mystery of the world we live in.

RACHEL CARSON

No matter how many challenges you face today, you can smile in the face of aggravation. How? By casting your cares upon the Lord. Yet many of us feel compelled to take all of the cares upon ourselves. We can handle anything that comes our way, right? Wrong! But God can. When the day starts to go south, cast your cares on Him. He wants you to!

MICHELLE MEDLOCK ADAMS

Do you ever fall asleep during your prayer sessions? As moms (especially new moms), we get so few hours of sleep that once we're still for a few moments, we tend to fall asleep. Ask God to help you be alert during your prayer periods. He will help you. And even if you still fall asleep, God won't be offended. He will be waiting when you wake up.

MICHELLE MEDLOCK ADAMS

One day, when your children are grown
and gone, you'll have time for a perfect house.
What matters now is not the house,
but the home; and not the children's duties,
but the children.

LINDA DAVIS ZUMBEHL

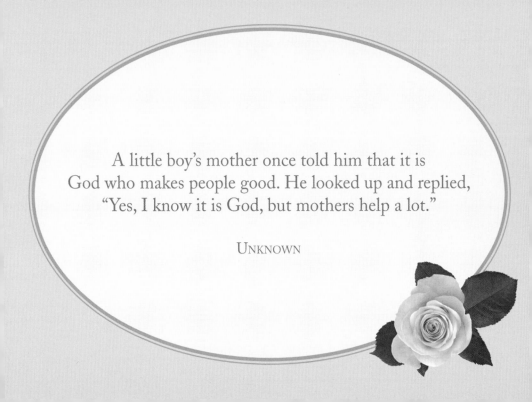

A little boy's mother once told him that it is
God who makes people good. He looked up and replied,
"Yes, I know it is God, but mothers help a lot."

UNKNOWN

Her children arise up,
and call her blessed;
her husband also,
and he praiseth her.

PROVERBS 31:28 KJV

Instead of focusing on the yucky part of cleanup, remember that the dirty pots and pans, the sticky table, the crumbs on the floor. . .all mean that you have a family who needs your love and care. Now doesn't that just make it all worthwhile?

FROM *IN THE KITCHEN WITH MARY AND MARTHA*

A good mother laughs our laughs,
sheds our tears, returns our love, fears our fears.
She lives our joys, cares our cares, and all our
hopes and dreams she shares.

UNKNOWN

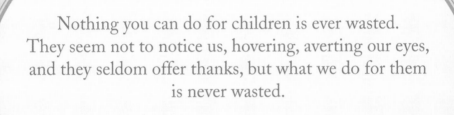

Nothing you can do for children is ever wasted.
They seem not to notice us, hovering, averting our eyes,
and they seldom offer thanks, but what we do for them
is never wasted.

GARRISON KEILLOR

Dear Father, help me to give You everything today: the things I do well—and the things at which I fail. Empower me to accept my circumstances, even life's daily frustrations. Thank You that when I am weak, You are strong. Amen.

ELLYN SANNA

Most of all the other beautiful things in life come by twos and threes, by dozens and hundreds. Plenty of roses, stars, sunsets, rainbows, brothers and sisters, aunts and cousins, but only one mother in the whole world.

KATE DOUGLAS WIGGIN

Mother—in this consists the glory and the most precious ornament of woman.

MARTIN LUTHER

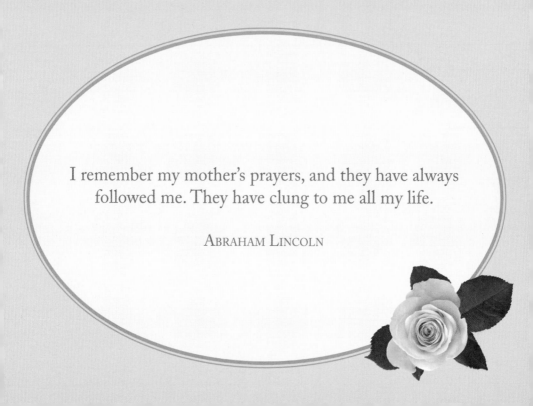

I remember my mother's prayers, and they have always followed me. They have clung to me all my life.

ABRAHAM LINCOLN

As moms, we can't run on empty love tanks. We are expected to give love all day long. If your love tank is low today, pull up to the Word of God and spend some time with the Lord. His love is waiting for you, and it's premium stuff. Ready? Begin fueling.

MICHELLE MEDLOCK ADAMS

The painter has with his brush transferred the landscape to the canvas with such fidelity that the trees and grasses seem almost real; he has made even the face of a maiden seem instinct with life, but there is one picture so beautiful that no painter has ever been able perfectly to reproduce it, and that is the picture of the mother holding in her arms her babe.

WILLIAM JENNINGS BRYAN

A mother's heart is always
with her children.

PROVERB

*Mother is the name for God in the lips
and hearts of little children.*

WILLIAM M. THACKERAY

*A mother is the truest
friend we have.*

WASHINGTON IRVING

Motherhood:
All love begins and ends there.

ROBERT BROWNING

There was never a woman like her.
She was gentle as a dove and brave
as a lioness.

ANDREW JACKSON

As one whom his mother comforteth,
so will I comfort you, [says the Lord].

ISAIAH 66:13 KJV

My mother was the source from which I derived the guiding principles of my life.

<small>JOHN WESLEY</small>

The memory of my mother will always be a blessing to me.

Thomas A. Edison

Thank you, God, for pretending not to notice that one of your angels is missing and for guiding her to me. Sometimes I wonder what special name you had for her. I call her "Mother."

Bernice Maddux

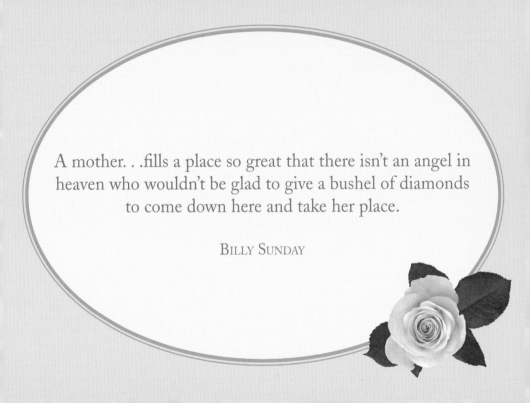

A mother. . .fills a place so great that there isn't an angel in heaven who wouldn't be glad to give a bushel of diamonds to come down here and take her place.

BILLY SUNDAY

As moms, we're sometimes afraid to trust God with our children. But what we fail to realize is this—He loves them even more than we do. He loved them before we ever held them in our arms. We can trust Him with our kids.

MICHELLE MEDLOCK ADAMS

A mother's love is indeed the golden link that binds youth to age; and he is still but a child who can yet recall, with a softened heart, the fond devotion, or the gentle chidings, of the best friend that God ever gives us.

CHRISTIAN NESTELL BOVEE

There is religion in all deep love, but the love of a mother is the veil of a softer light, between the heart and the heavenly Father.

SAMUEL TAYLOR COLERIDGE

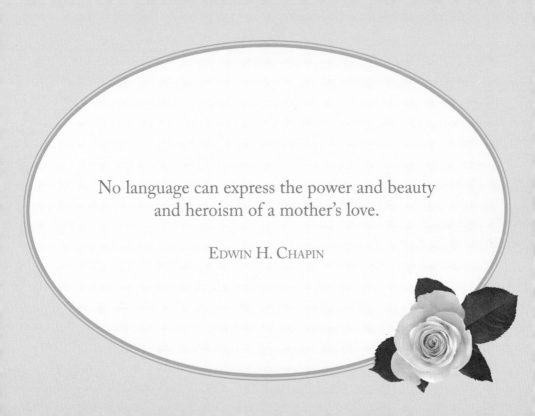

No language can express the power and beauty
and heroism of a mother's love.

Edwin H. Chapin

Mother means selfless devotion, limitless sacrifice, and love that passes understanding.

UNKNOWN

Mother love is the fuel that enables normal
human beings to do the impossible.

Marion C. Garrety

A mother is one who is
still there when everyone
else has deserted you.

UNKNOWN

Through the ages no nation has had a better friend
than the mother who taught her child to pray.

Unknown

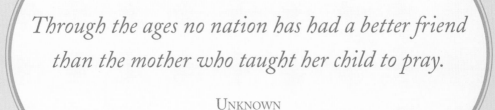

You may remember thinking, *I can't do this one more day! God must not have known what He was doing when He made me a mom.* But, you know what? He did know. He has equipped you with everything you need to be a good mom. And He is more than happy to help you through when you feel your weakest. No matter what—God loves you and believes in you.

MICHELLE MEDLOCK ADAMS

There is in every true woman's heart a spark of heavenly fire, which lies dormant in the broad daylight of prosperity, but which kindles up and beams and blazes in the dark hour of adversity.

WASHINGTON IRVING

May your father and mother be glad;
may she who gave you birth rejoice!

PROVERBS 23:25 NIV

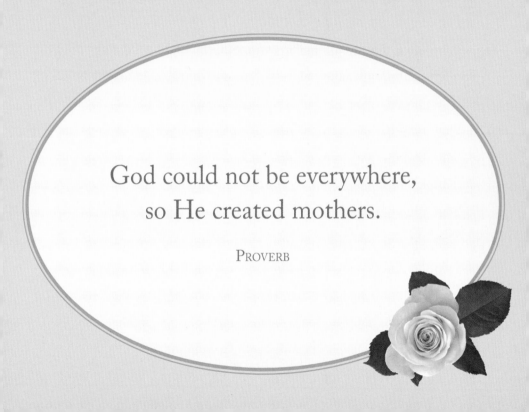

God could not be everywhere,
so He created mothers.

PROVERB

Motherhood is priced of God,
At price no man may dare
To lessen or misunderstand.

HELEN HUNT JACKSON

The hand that rocks the cradle
is the hand that rules the world.

WILLIAM ROSS WALLACE

Even He that died for us upon the cross was mindful of His mother, as if to teach us that this holy love should be our last worldly thought.

HENRY WADSWORTH LONGFELLOW

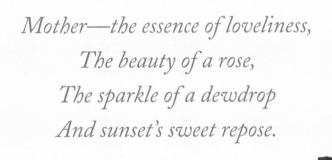

Mother—the essence of loveliness,
The beauty of a rose,
The sparkle of a dewdrop
And sunset's sweet repose.

LYDIA M. JOHNSON

To a child's ear,
"mother" is magic
in any language.

ARLENE BENEDICT

The imprint of the mother remains
forever on the life of a child.

GERMAN PROVERB

[My mother] is my first, great love. She was a wonderful, rare woman as strong and steadfast and generous as the sun. She could be as kind and gentle as warm rain and as steadfast as the irreducible earth beneath us.

D. H. Lawrence

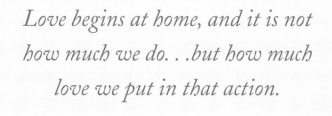

Love begins at home, and it is not how much we do. . .but how much love we put in that action.

MOTHER TERESA

Motherhood is a
partnership with God.

UNKNOWN

A hundred men may make an encampment,
but it takes a woman to make a home.

CHINESE PROVERB

A mother is she who can take the place of all others but whose place no one else can take.

CARDINAL MERMILLOD

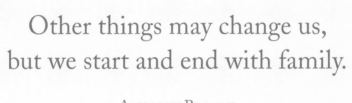

Other things may change us,
but we start and end with family.

ANTHONY BRANDT

Mother, you wrote no lofty
poems that critics consider art;
But with a nobler vision you have
lived them in your heart.

THOMAS FESSENDEN

"When a woman gives birth, she has a hard time, there's no getting around it. But when the baby is born, there is joy in the birth. This new life in the world wipes out the memory of the pain."

JOHN 16:21 MSG

She has achieved success who has lived well,
laughed often, and loved much.

BESSIE ANDERSON TANLEY

Mother—that was the bank where
we deposited all our hurts and worries.

T. DeWitt Talmage

A mother's love is unconditional
and will touch a child's heart for
years to come.

WANDA E. BRUNSTETTER

Loving motherhood and prayer are two concepts that work best in tandem.

SYLVIA GLEASON

There is no love on earth, I think, as potent and enduring as a mother's love for her child.

ANN KIEMEL ANDERSON

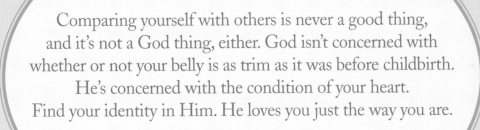

Comparing yourself with others is never a good thing,
and it's not a God thing, either. God isn't concerned with
whether or not your belly is as trim as it was before childbirth.
He's concerned with the condition of your heart.
Find your identity in Him. He loves you just the way you are.

MICHELLE MEDLOCK ADAMS

A mother's love is so strong and unyielding that it usually endures all circumstances: good fortune and misfortune, prosperity and privation, honor and disgrace.

UNKNOWN

I affirm my profound belief that God's greatest creation is womanhood. I also believe that there is no greater good in all the world than motherhood. The influence of a mother in the lives of her children is beyond calculation.

JAMES E. FAUST

You may have others who will be more
demonstrative but never who will love you more
unselfishly than your mother or who will be
willing to do or bear more for your good.

CATHERINE BRAMWELL BOOTH

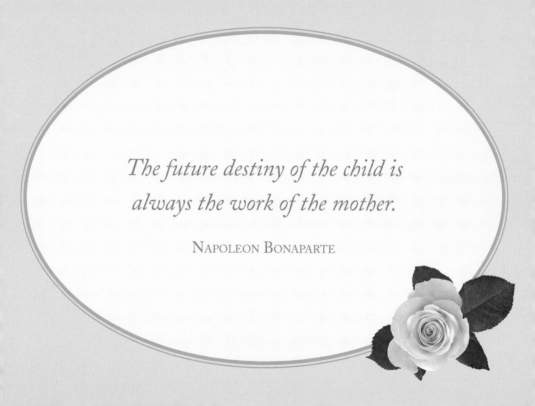

The future destiny of the child is always the work of the mother.

Napoleon Bonaparte

*Love comforteth like
sunshine after rain.*

WILLIAM SHAKESPEARE

Mother's love grows by giving.

CHARLES LAMB

She is the guardian of the family, the queen, the tender hand of love. A mother is the best friend anyone ever had. A mother is love.

UNKNOWN

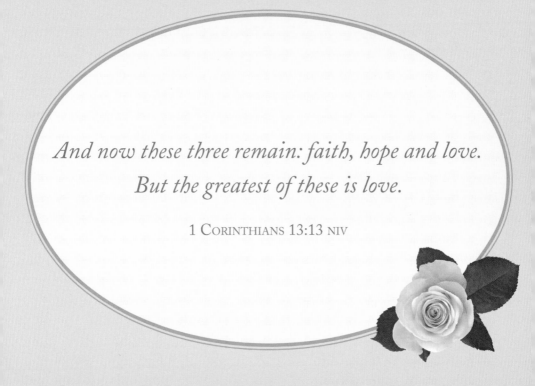

And now these three remain: faith, hope and love.
But the greatest of these is love.

1 CORINTHIANS 13:13 NIV

*There are times when only a
mother's faith
can help us on life's way,
And inspire in us the confidence
we need from day to day.*

UNKNOWN

The Christian home is the Master's workshop where
the process of character molding is silently, lovingly,
faithfully, and successfully carried on.

LORD HOUGHTON

There is no more influential or powerful role on earth than a mother's. Their words are never fully forgotten, their touch leaves an indelible impression, and the memory of their presence lasts a lifetime.

CHARLES SWINDOLL

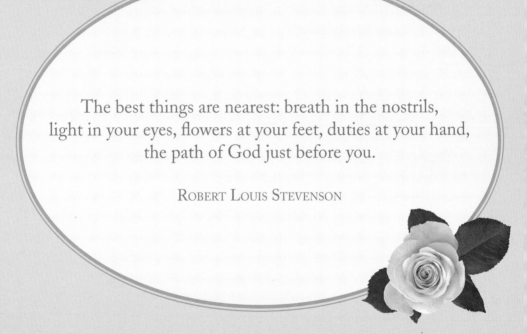

The best things are nearest: breath in the nostrils,
light in your eyes, flowers at your feet, duties at your hand,
the path of God just before you.

ROBERT LOUIS STEVENSON

Children are the sum of
what mothers contribute
to their lives.

UNKNOWN

Guide me, O Lord, in all the changes and varieties of the world; that in all things that shall happen I may have an evenness and tranquility of spirit; that my soul may be wholly resigned to Thy divine will and pleasure.

JEREMY TAYLOR

Blessed are the flexible, for they shall bend and not break!

UNKNOWN

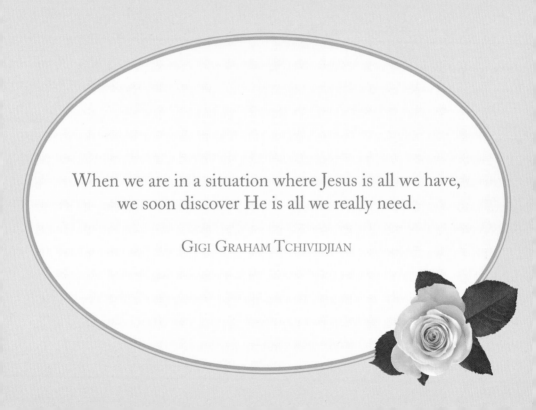

When we are in a situation where Jesus is all we have,
we soon discover He is all we really need.

GIGI GRAHAM TCHIVIDJIAN

To be a mother is a woman's greatest vocation in life. She is a partner with God.

SPENCER W. KIMBALL

Be the living expression of God's kindness: kindness in your face, kindness in your eyes, kindness in your smile.

MOTHER TERESA

Becoming a mother makes you the mother of all children. You long to comfort all who are desolate.

CHARLOTTE GRAY

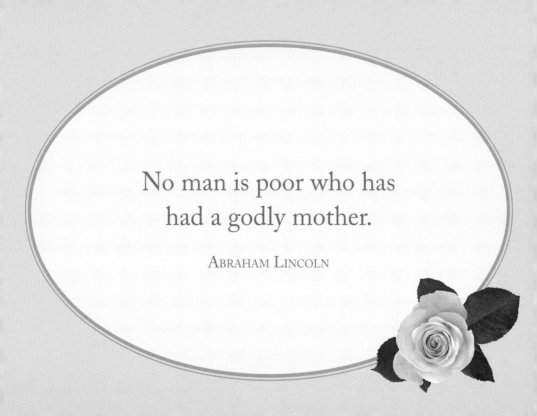

No man is poor who has
had a godly mother.

ABRAHAM LINCOLN

The heart of a mother is a deep abyss at the bottom of which you will always find forgiveness.

HONORÉ DE BALZAC

Father, transform my thinking.
Help me to quit worrying and simply
trust You with every part of my life.

MICHELLE MEDLOCK ADAMS

There is no influence so powerful
as that of the mother.

SARAH JOSEPHA HALE

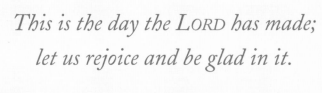

This is the day the LORD has made;
let us rejoice and be glad in it.

PSALM 118:24 NIV

*Her dignity consists in being
unknown to the world;
her glory is in the esteem of her
husband; her pleasures in the
happiness of her family.*

JEAN ROUSEAU

Everybody knows that a good mother gives her children
a feeling of trust and stability. She is the one they can
count on for the things that matter most of all.

KATHARINE BUTLER HATHAWAY

There is no friendship, no love,
like that of the mother for the child.

Henry Ward Beecher

*Be kind to thy mother,
for when thou were young,
who loved thee so fondly as she?*

MARGARET COURTNEY

Stories first heard at a mother's knee are never wholly forgotten—a little spring that never quite dries up in our journey through scorching years.

GIOVANNI RUFFINI

In life, you just can't plan for everything.
But remember—while you can't plan for
everything, God can. He has a plan for your life,
so don't sweat the small stuff.

MICHELLE MEDLOCK ADAMS

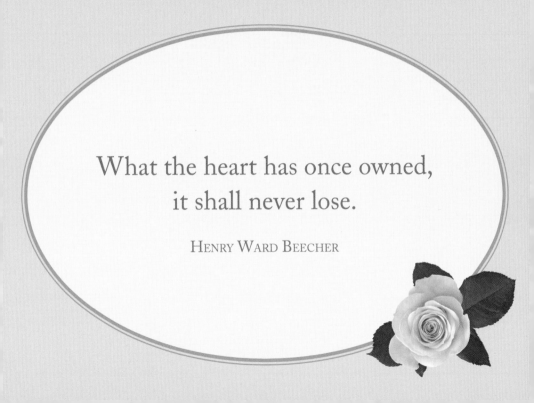

What the heart has once owned,
it shall never lose.

HENRY WARD BEECHER

Duty makes us do things well,
but love makes us do them
beautifully.

PHILLIPS BROOKS

An instant of pure love is more precious to God. . .
than all other good works together.

JOHN OF THE CROSS

Isn't it amazing how much you loved the baby you were carrying even though you'd never actually met that little person? To think that God knew me before I was ever born—wow! . . . If you are struggling with a poor self-image today, snap out of it! You've been approved by Almighty God!

MICHELLE MEDLOCK ADAMS

A mother's love is instinctual,
unconditional, and forever.

UNKNOWN

They are angels of
God in disguise;
His sunlight still gleams
in their tresses;
His glory still gleams
in their eyes.

CHARLES M. DICKINSON

My mother's hands are cool and fair,
they can do anything.
Delicate mercies hid them there
like flowers in the spring.

ANNA HEMPSTEAD BRANCH

By the grace of God I am what I am;
and his grace which was bestowed upon
me was not in vain; but I laboured more
abundantly than they all: yet not I,
but the grace of God which was with me.

1 CORINTHIANS 15:10 KJV

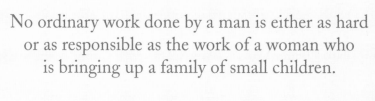

No ordinary work done by a man is either as hard
or as responsible as the work of a woman who
is bringing up a family of small children.

THEODORE ROOSEVELT

*God puts each fresh morning,
each new chance of life, into our
hands as a gift to see what we
will do with it.*

Unknown

It may be one more request than we think we can fulfill,
one more responsibility than we think we can manage. . . .
Interruptions never distracted Jesus. He accepted them
as opportunities of a richer service.

RUTH BELL GRAHAM

There is nothing outside
the reach of God.

BARBARA JOHNSON

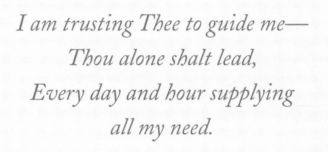

I am trusting Thee to guide me—
Thou alone shalt lead,
Every day and hour supplying
all my need.

FRANCES RIDLEY HAVERGAL

We have a life expert always on the job—God. The next time you get overloaded with the cares of the world, call on Him. He will take care of everything, and He doesn't even charge a commission!

MICHELLE MEDLOCK ADAMS

Beauty—when you look
into a woman's eyes and see
what is in her heart.

NATE DIRCKS

It's not how much we have,
but how much we enjoy,
that makes happiness.

CHARLES SPURGEON

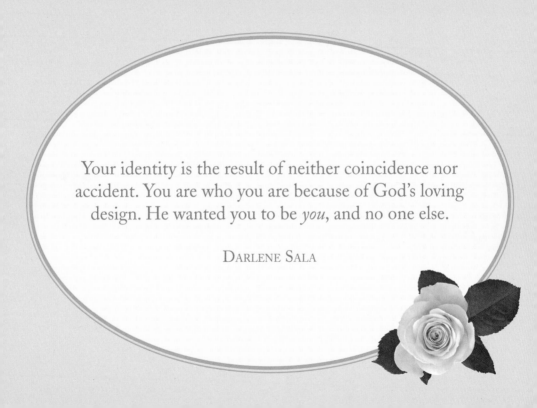

Your identity is the result of neither coincidence nor accident. You are who you are because of God's loving design. He wanted you to be *you*, and no one else.

DARLENE SALA

You will find that as you look back upon your life that the moments when you have truly lived are the moments when you have done things in the spirit of love.

HENRY DRUMMOND